Pebble® Plus

AFRICAN ANIMALS
Elephants

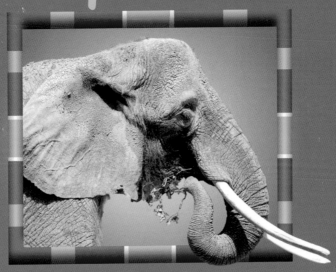

by Sydnie Meltzer Kleinhenz

Consulting Editor: Gail Saunders-Smith, PhD

Consultant:
George Wittemyer, PhD
NSF International Postdoctoral Fellow
University of California at Berkeley

Capstone
press

Mankato, Minnesota

Pebble Plus is published by Capstone Press,
151 Good Counsel Drive, P.O. Box 669, Mankato, Minnesota 56002.
www.capstonepress.com

1 2 3 4 5 6 13 12 11 10 09 08

Library of Congress Cataloging-in-Publication Data
Meltzer Kleinhenz, Sydnie.
    Elephants / by Sydnie Meltzer Kleinhenz.
    p. cm. — (Pebble plus. African animals)
    Includes bibliographical references and index.
    ISBN-13: 978-1-4296-1245-6 (hardcover)
    ISBN-10: 1-4296-1245-2 (hardcover)
    1. Elephants — Africa — Juvenile literature. I. Title. II. Series.
QL737.P98M43 2008
599.67'4 — dc22   2007028675

Summary: Discusses elephants, their African habitat, food, and behavior.

Editorial Credits
Erika L. Shores, editor; Renée T. Doyle, set designer; Laura Manthe, photo researcher

Photo Credits
Afripics.com, 6–7, 8–9
Digital Vision/Gerry Ellis, 16–17
Dreamstime/Chris Fourie, 10–11; Nicole Kuehl, 20–21
Gary W. Sargent, 5
iStockphoto/Beverly Guhl Davis, 22
Photodisc/Siede Preis, cover, 1, 3 (skin)
Shutterstock/EcoPrint, 18–19; Jody Dingle, 1; Neil Wigmore, 15; Vera Bogaerts, 12–13; Victor Soares, cover

Note to Parents and Teachers

The African Animals set supports national science standards related to life science.
This book describes and illustrates elephants. The images support early readers in
understanding the text. The repetition of words and phrases helps early readers learn
new words. This book also introduces early readers to subject-specific vocabulary words,
which are defined in the Glossary section. Early readers may need assistance to read
some words and to use the Table of Contents, Glossary, Read More, Internet Sites, and
Index sections of the book.

Table of Contents

Living in Africa 4

Up Close! 8

Eating and Drinking. 14

Staying Safe 20

Glossary 22

Read More 23

Internet Sites. 23

Index 24

Living in Africa

The biggest land animals

live in Africa.

Elephants roam

the grassy savanna.

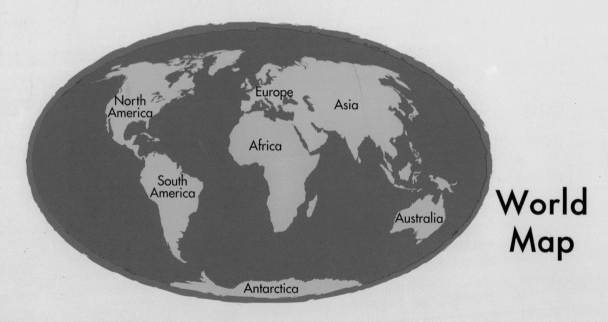

World Map

North America

Europe

Asia

Africa

South America

Australia

Antarctica

The savanna is hot.

Elephants shower themselves

with cool water.

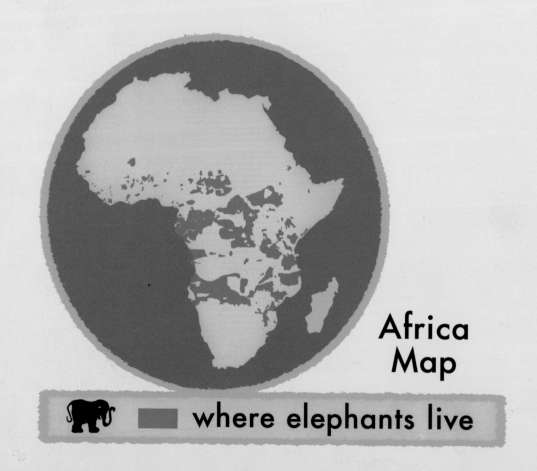

Africa
Map

where elephants live

Up Close!

Wrinkly elephant skin

can get a sunburn.

Elephants roll in mud.

The mud works like sunscreen.

An elephant's trunk

is more than a nose.

Elephants play and

give hugs with their trunks.

Elephants grow two
jumbo teeth called tusks.
Elephants use their tusks
to break branches.

13

Eating and Drinking

Elephants eat all day.

Their trunks grab branches,

leaves, and grass.

Some months are dry
on the savanna.
Elephants must walk far
to find food and water.

Mothers teach calves
to use their trunks.
Calves learn to blow water
into their mouths.

Staying Safe

Calves stay near their mothers.

The herd keeps them

safe at night.

Good night, elephants.

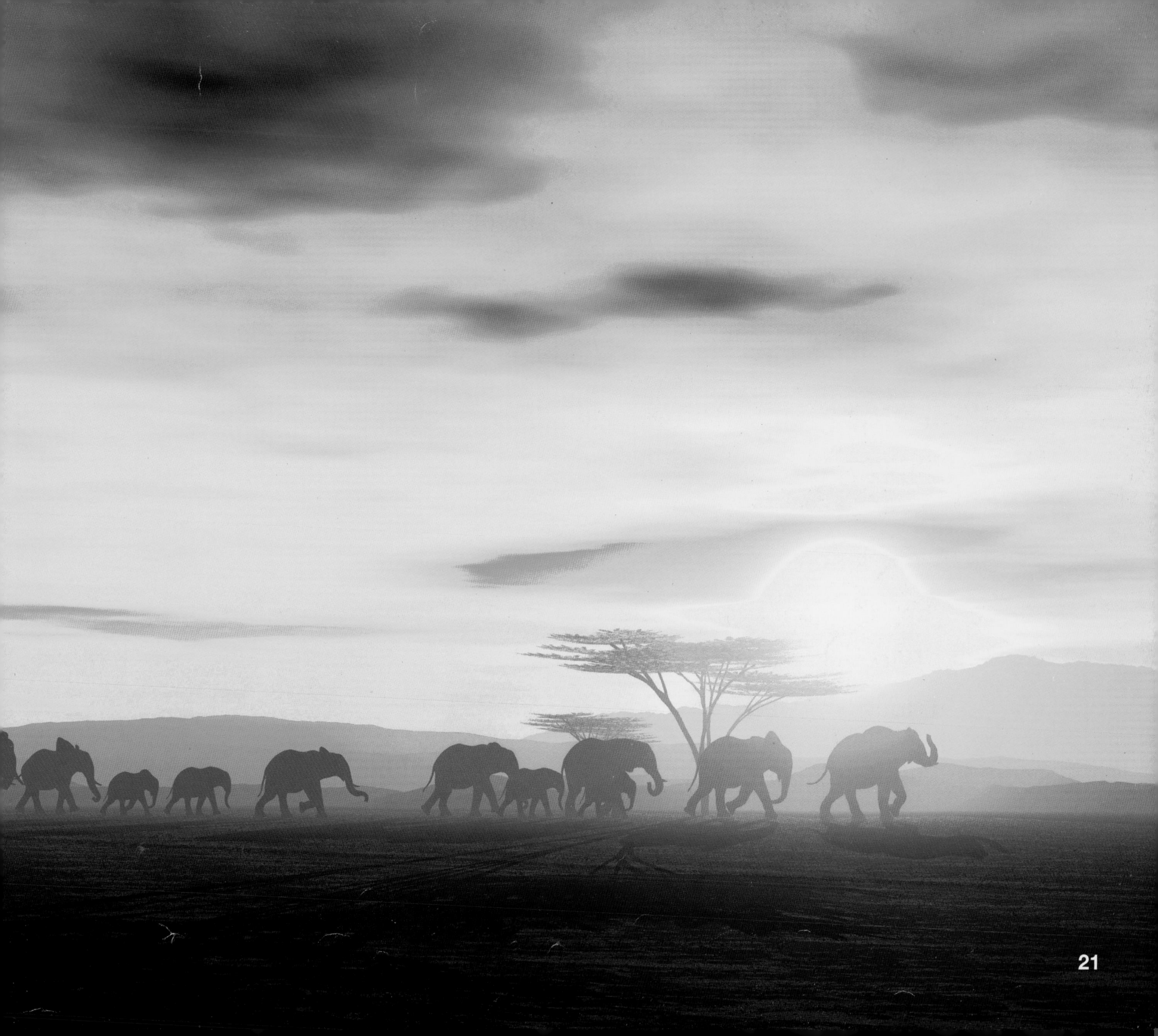

Glossary

calf — a young elephant

herd — a group of elephants; an elephant herd is made up of related female elephants and their young; male elephants live on their own.

roam — to wander

savanna — a flat, grassy plain with few trees

sunburn — sore skin caused by staying in the sun too long

sunscreen — lotion that prevents sunburn

trunk — an elephant's nose; elephants use their trunk like a hand.

tusk — a long, curved, pointed tooth

Read More

Bredeson, Carmen. *African Elephants Up Close.* Zoom in on Animals! Berkeley Heights, N.J.: Enslow, 2006.

Hall, Margaret. *Elephants and Their Calves.* Animal Offspring. Mankato, Minn.: Capstone Press, 2004.

Knudsen, Shannon. *African Elephants.* Pull Ahead Books. Minneapolis: Lerner, 2006.

Internet Sites

FactHound offers a safe, fun way to find Internet sites related to this book. All of the sites on FactHound have been researched by our staff.

Here's how:

1. Visit *www.facthound.com*

2. Choose your grade level.

3. Type in this book ID **1429612452** for age-appropriate sites. You may also browse subjects by clicking on letters, or by clicking on pictures and words.

4. Click on the **Fetch It** button.

FactHound will fetch the best sites for you!

Index

Africa, 4

calves, 18, 20

food, 14, 16

grass, 4, 14

herds, 20

mothers, 18, 20

mud, 8

night, 20

playing, 10

savanna, 4, 6, 16

skin, 8

sunburn, 8

trunks, 10, 14

tusks, 12

walking, 16

water, 6, 16, 18

Word Count: 125
Grade: 1
Early-Intervention Level: 18